30

MINUTES
OR LESS

Fresh
Food

30
MINUTES
OR LESS

Fresh
Food

p

This is a Parragon Publishing Book

First published in 2006

Parragon Publishing

Queen Street House

4 Queen Street

Bath BA1 1HE, UK

Copyright © Parragon Books Ltd 2006

ISBN: 1-40547-307-X

Printed in China

Produced by the Bridgewater Book Company Ltd

Front cover photography by Laurie Evans
Front cover home economy by Carol Tennant

Notes for the Reader

This book uses imperial, metric, and US cup measurements. Follow the same units of measurement throughout; do not mix imperial and metric. All spoon measurements are level: teaspoons are assumed to be 5 ml, and tablespoons are assumed to be 15 ml. Unless otherwise stated, milk is assumed to be whole, eggs and individual vegetables are medium, and pepper is freshly ground black pepper.

Recipes using raw or very lightly cooked eggs should be avoided by infants, the elderly, pregnant women, convalescents, and anyone suffering from an illness. Pregnant women and breast-feeding women are advised to avoid eating peanuts and peanut products.

Contents

Introduction

This book is written for all those who enjoy eating good food but lack the time to spend hours in the kitchen. Cooking isn't rocket science nor is it only for the super-skilled—anyone with some fresh ingredients and a few pots and pans can produce something good to eat, and quickly, too. All the recipes in this book can be completed in 30 minutes or less.

Fast food is not just about burgers, french fries, or hotdogs—fast food can mean a sliver of top-quality prosciutto wrapped around a slice of perfectly ripe melon. Fresh food makes fabulous fast food—and if you cook it as little as possible, you'll benefit from the maximum amount of nutrients that the ingredients possess.

The book is divided into four chapters: Snacks and Appetizers, Main Courses, Salads, and Desserts, giving you the option of preparing simple meals for everyday eating or serving up a dinner party feast with the minimum of time and effort. Recipes have been inspired by regional cuisines from around the world, drawing on a wealth of flavors to tantalize your taste buds and satisfy your appetite.

CHOOSING FRESH FOOD

If you spend a little time selecting good-quality ingredients, you'll really notice the difference on your plate. This doesn't mean you've always got to buy the best organic produce at a premium price—there's plenty of quality fresh food on offer at your local supermarket. The key to identifying truly fresh food is that it looks good and smells good, too. Here are a few pointers as to what to look for and how to store it:

Meat: meat should never be slimy nor should it smell. Exposed bones should be a pinkish-blue color and any fat on the meat should be pale. If tightly wrapped, pierce the plastic wrap and store at the bottom of the refrigerator for no more than two days.

Dairy produce: milk and yogurt will keep if covered and refrigerated for up to three days. Unsalted butter will keep for two weeks; salted for one month as long as it is refrigerated and tightly wrapped. The freshness of cheese depends on whether it's hard or soft and the ripeness of it when purchased. To keep at its best, wrap in plastic wrap and remove from the refrigerator an hour before serving.

Fish: fish must be bought and consumed when it's still very fresh—it shouldn't smell and it should have bright eyes, red gills, and firm flesh. It's always best to buy fish off the slab rather than pre-packed. Your fish-dealer will bone, scale, clean, and fillet the fish for you if you don't fancy doing this yourself (it saves your time, too). Refrigerate and eat on the day of purchase.

Vegetables: always choose vegetables that are young and fresh. They should be brightly colored, unwrinkled, and unblemished. Unwrap anything that comes in cellophane and store in the salad compartment of the refrigerator or in a larder. If there is no room in the refrigerator, do not keep vegetables in your kitchen in plastic bags because they will sweat and rot.

Fruit: fruit should be bright-skinned and have a strong scent without being overpowering. Some fruit, such as pears, are rarely in perfect condition in the stores because they are completely ripe only for one day—they should therefore be bought in advance and ripened at home. Don't store soft fruit for more than two days in a refrigerator and do not prepare until ready for use. Citrus and hard fruit will stay fresh for up to a few weeks.

The recipes in this book are all based on fresh food, and there are no complicated cooking methods or elaborate presentations, nor will you need to use every pot and pan in the kitchen. Whether it's a simple Mixed Herb Omelet, a tasty Grilled Steak with Tomatoes and Garlic, a tangy Traditional Greek Salad, or fragrant Baked Peaches, there's nothing to match the eating experience of real fresh food.

Chapter One
Snacks and Appetizers

Tomato Bread
5 minutes to the table

SERVES 4

ingredients

6-8 slices French bread or other
   crusty loaf
3-4 tomatoes, halved
1-2 garlic cloves, halved (optional)
extra-virgin olive oil, for drizzling
   (optional)

method

To prepare this at its simplest, rub the bread slices with the cut sides of the tomato halves, letting the juice and seeds soak into the bread. If the bread is too soft, you can lightly toast it beforehand.

Other options are to flavor the bread slices with garlic by rubbing with the garlic halves in the same way, or drizzle extra-virgin olive oil over the top of the tomatoes.

variation

To make a more substantial snack, serve the bread with a plate of thinly sliced serrano ham and sheep-milk cheese, and let guests assemble open sandwiches for themselves.

Mixed Herb Omelet
15 minutes to the table

SERVES 1

ingredients

2 large eggs

2 tbsp milk

3 tbsp butter

1 fresh flat-leaf parsley sprig,
   stem bruised

leaves from 1 fresh flat-leaf
   parsley sprig

1 fresh chervil sprig

2 fresh chives, chopped

salt and pepper

method

Break the eggs into a bowl. Add the milk and salt and pepper to taste, and quickly beat until just blended.

Heat an 8-inch/20-cm omelet pan or skillet over medium-high heat until very hot and you can feel the heat rising from the surface. Add 2 tablespoons of the butter and use a fork to rub it over the bottom and around the side of the pan as it melts.

As soon as the butter stops sizzling, pour in the eggs. Shake the pan forward and backward over the heat and use the fork to stir the eggs around the pan in a circular motion. Do not scrape the bottom of the pan.

As the omelet begins to set, use the fork to push the cooked egg from the edge toward the center, so that the remaining uncooked egg comes in contact with the hot bottom of the pan. Continue doing this for 3 minutes, or until the omelet looks set on the bottom but is still slightly runny on top.

Put the herbs in the center of the omelet. Tilt the pan away from the handle, so that the omelet slides toward the edge of the pan. Use the fork to fold the top half of the omelet over the herbs. Slide the omelet onto a plate, then rub the remaining butter over the top. Serve immediately.

Shrimp Toasts
20 minutes to the table

method

Pound the shrimp to a pulp in a mortar with a pestle or with the bottom of a cleaver.

Mix the shrimp with one of the egg whites and half the cornstarch in a bowl. Add the sugar and salt, and stir in the cilantro. Mix the remaining egg white with the remaining cornstarch in a pitcher.

Remove the crusts from the bread and cut each slice into 8 triangles. Brush the top of each piece with the egg white and cornstarch mixture, then add 1 teaspoon of the shrimp mixture and spread smoothly over the top.

Heat enough oil for deep-frying in a wok, deep-fat fryer, or large, heavy-bottomed pan until it reaches 350–375°F/180–190°C, or until a cube of bread browns in 30 seconds. Without overcrowding the wok, cook the toasts shrimp-side up for 2 minutes. Turn and cook for an additional 2 minutes, or until beginning to turn golden brown. Remove with a slotted spoon, then drain on paper towels and keep warm in a low oven while cooking the remainder.

MAKES 16

ingredients

3½ oz/100 g raw shrimp, shelled and deveined

2 egg whites

2 tbsp cornstarch

½ tsp sugar

pinch of salt

2 tbsp finely chopped fresh cilantro leaves

2 slices day-old white bread

vegetable or peanut oil, for deep-frying

Soba Noodle Rolls
30 minutes to the table

MAKES 24

ingredients

4 oz/115 g sushi-grade tuna or piece
   of tuna fillet

1 tbsp oil (if using tuna fillet)

3½ oz/100 g soba noodles, broken
   into pieces

1 scallion, green part only, thinly sliced

1 tbsp light soy sauce

½ tbsp rice vinegar

pinch of wasabi paste

1 tbsp pickled ginger, finely chopped

6 small sheets toasted nori

½ cucumber, peeled and finely
   shredded

method

If using a piece of tuna fillet, heat the oil in a skillet and sear the tuna all over for 6 minutes, or until almost cooked through. Cut the sushi-grade tuna or cooked tuna into strips.

Meanwhile, cook the soba noodles in a pan of boiling water until just cooked through, then drain and rinse under cold running water. Drain thoroughly. Gently mix the noodles with the scallion, soy sauce, vinegar, wasabi, and pickled ginger in a bowl.

Divide the noodle mixture into 6 equal portions. Put a sheet of nori shiny-side down on a rolling mat with the longest end toward you and mound a portion of the noodle mixture on the bottom third of the nori. Lay a sixth of the cucumber on top, then a layer of tuna strips.

To roll the sushi, fold the mat over, starting at the end where the ingredients are and tucking in the end of the nori to start the roll. Keep rolling, lifting up the mat as you go and keeping the pressure even but gentle until you have finished the roll. Moisten the top edge of the nori with water to seal the sushi roll closed. Don't worry if anything falls out of the sides—just push it back in.

Remove the roll from the mat and cut into 4 even-size pieces with a wet, very sharp knife. Turn the pieces on end and arrange them on a plate. Repeat with the remaining ingredients.

cook's tip

Lay the bamboo rolling mat on a cutting board with bamboo strips going horizontally from you and place on plastic wrap before rolling.

Pear and Roquefort Open-Face Sandwiches
15 minutes to the table

MAKES 4

ingredients

4 slices walnut bread, about
   ½ inch/1 cm thick
4 thin slices cured ham, such as
   Bayonne or prosciutto
2 ripe pears, such as Conference,
   peeled, halved, cored, and thinly
   sliced lengthwise
3½ oz/100 g Roquefort cheese, very
   thinly sliced
mixed salad greens, washed and dried,
   to serve

WALNUT VINAIGRETTE
½ cup walnut oil
3 tbsp white wine vinegar or lemon
   juice
1 tsp Dijon mustard
½ tsp superfine sugar
salt and pepper
2 tbsp chopped walnuts

method

To make the vinaigrette, put all ingredients in a jar, then blend using a stick blender until a thick emulsion forms. Alternatively, put all the ingredients in a screw-top jar, then secure the lid and shake vigorously until the emulsion forms. Taste and adjust the seasoning if necessary.

Preheat the broiler to high. Toast the bread slices on both sides under the preheated broiler until crisp but not brown. Do not turn off the broiler.

Fold or cut the ham slices to cover each slice of bread, then divide the pear slices equally between the bread slices. Lay the cheese slices on top.

Return the bread slices to the broiler and cook until the cheese melts and bubbles. Mix the salad greens with the walnut vinaigrette and serve 1 or 2 sandwiches per person with the salad on the side.

variations

For a crunchy snack in a flash, spread slices of sourdough bread with salted butter and top with thinly sliced new-season radishes and a sprinkling of finely chopped fresh parsley. For a quick alternative to a traditional Croque Monsieur, top toasted bread slices with cooked ham and thin slices of bleu cheese, and broil until the cheese melts and bubbles. Spread thick slices of untoasted bread with salted butter and top with a selection of thinly sliced cooked or smoked sausages.

Steamed Spring Rolls
25 minutes to the table

method

Put the wrappers between 2 dampened dish towels and let stand for 2 minutes, or until soft. Alternatively, soak them in warm water and lift out one at a time to work on. Meanwhile, cook the vermicelli noodles in a pan of boiling water until just cooked through, then drain and rinse under cold running water. Drain thoroughly.

Put 1-2 basil leaves in the center of a wrapper and top with a little chili sauce. Arrange 2 shrimp on top and then some of the scallion and carrot. Add a few noodles and roll up. Flip one edge of the wrapper over the filling, then fold the sides over to enclose and roll up. Repeat with the remaining wrapper and filling.

Arrange the filled wrapper in a single layer in the top of a steamer. Cook over simmering water for 4-5 minutes, or until heated through. Serve immediately with extra chili sauce for dipping.

MAKES 12

ingredients

12 rice flour wrappers

2 oz/55 g rice vermicelli noodles

12-24 fresh Thai basil leaves

2 tbsp chili sauce, plus extra
  to serve

24 cooked and shelled jumbo shrimp

4 scallions, cut into thin strips

1 carrot, cut into short thin sticks

Broiled Eggplant with Provolone and Tapenade

30 minutes to the table

SERVES 4

ingredients

1 large eggplant, thinly sliced
    lengthwise
5 tbsp olive oil
scant ½ cup black olives, pitted
1 tbsp capers
2 tbsp chopped fresh flat-leaf parsley
1¾ oz/50 g sun-dried tomatoes in oil
    (drained weight)
2 garlic cloves
1 tsp lemon juice
6 oz/175 g provolone cheese,
    cut into sticks

method

Preheat the oven to 425°F/220°C. Brush the eggplant slices with 2 tablespoons of the oil and place on a cookie sheet. Bake the eggplants in the preheated oven for 10 minutes, or until soft. Let cool.

Meanwhile, for the tapenade, put the olives, capers, half the parsley, the tomatoes, and garlic in a food processor and pulse until coarsely chopped, or coarsely chop by hand. Add 2 tablespoons of the remaining oil and the lemon juice, then pulse again to form a smooth paste, or beat into the olive mixture by hand.

Preheat the broiler to high. When the eggplant slices are cool enough to handle, spread each one with a little of the tapenade. Put a couple of the cheese sticks at the end of each eggplant slice, then roll up and secure with a toothpick.

Brush the eggplant rolls with the remaining oil and cook under the preheated broiler, turning once, until golden brown and the cheese is beginning to melt. Serve scattered with the remaining parsley.

Broiled Sardines with Lemon Sauce

30 minutes to the table

SERVES 4

ingredients

2 tbsp unsalted butter
12 fresh sardines, cleaned, scaled (see
    cook's tip), and heads removed
salt and pepper

LEMON SAUCE
1 large lemon
scant 2 tbsp unsalted butter
1 tbsp chopped fresh fennel leaves

method

Preheat the broiler or grill. Melt 2 tbsp of the butter in a small pan and season to taste with salt and pepper. Brush the sardines all over with the melted butter and cook under the preheated broiler or on the grill, turning once, for 5–6 minutes, or until cooked through.

To make the sauce, peel the lemon. Using a small, serrated knife, remove all the white pith from the lemon. Cut between the membranes and ease out the flesh segments, discarding any seeds. Chop finely and set aside. Melt the remaining butter in the pan, then remove from the heat. Stir in the chopped lemon and fennel.

Transfer the sardines to a warmed platter, then pour the sauce over and serve immediately.

cook's tip

To clean the sardines, slit open the belly and remove the insides. Rinse and dry. To scale, hold each fish in turn by its tail under cold running water and run your hand along the body from tail to head until the scales are removed.

Baked Zucchini

20 minutes to the table

method

Preheat the oven to 400°F/200°C.

Slice the zucchini lengthwise into 4 strips each. Brush with oil and place on a cookie sheet, or in an ovenproof dish.

Bake the zucchini in the oven for 10 minutes without letting them get too limp.

Remove the zucchini from the preheated oven. Arrange slices of cheese on top and sprinkle with diced tomato and chopped oregano. Return to the oven for 5 minutes or until the cheese melts.

Remove the zucchini from the oven and transfer carefully to serving plates, or serve straight from the baking dish, garnished with fresh basil leaves.

SERVES 4

ingredients

4 medium zucchini
2 tbsp extra-virgin olive oil
4 oz/115 g mozzarella cheese,
   thinly sliced
2 large tomatoes, seeded and diced
2 tsp chopped fresh oregano
a few fresh basil leaves, to garnish

Prosciutto with Arugula

10 minutes to the table

SERVES 4

ingredients

4 oz/115 g arugula

1 tbsp lemon juice

3 tbsp extra-virgin olive oil

8 oz/225 g prosciutto, thinly sliced

salt and pepper

method

Wash the arugula in cold water and pat dry with paper towels. Put the greens in a bowl.

Pour the lemon juice into a small bowl and season to taste with salt and pepper. Whisk in the oil, then pour the dressing over the arugula and toss lightly to coat.

Arrange the slices of prosciutto in folds on 4 individual serving plates, then divide the arugula equally between the plates. Serve at room temperature.

variations

For a more substantial salad, add 1 thinly sliced fennel bulb and 2 thinly sliced oranges to the arugula in the bowl at the beginning of the method. Substitute orange juice or balsamic vinegar for the lemon juice in the dressing.

Melon and Kiwifruit Bowl

10 minutes to the table

SERVES 2

ingredients

1 small Charentais, Cantaloupe, or
   Galia melon

2 kiwifruit

method

Cut the melon into fourths and remove and discard the seeds. Using a sharp knife, remove the melon flesh from the skin and cut into chunks. Put in a bowl.

   Peel the kiwifruit and cut the flesh into slices. Add to the melon and gently mix together. Cover and refrigerate until required or divide equally between 2 serving dishes and serve immediately.

Chapter Two
Main Courses

Chicken with Goat Cheese and Basil

25 minutes to the table

SERVES 4

ingredients

4 skinless, boneless chicken breasts,
   about 4 oz/115 g each
3½ oz/100 g soft goat cheese
small bunch of fresh basil, reserving
   sprigs for garnish
2 tbsp olive oil
salt and pepper

method

Using a sharp knife, slit along one long edge of each chicken breast, then carefully open out each breast to make a small pocket. Divide the goat cheese equally between the pockets and tuck 3-4 basil leaves in each, leaving the sprigs in reserve for a garnish. Close the openings and season the chicken breasts to taste with salt and pepper.

   Heat the oil in a large skillet, then add the chicken breasts and cook gently for 15-20 minutes, turning several times, until golden and tender, and the juices run clear when a skewer is inserted into the thickest part of the meat. Serve warm, garnished with the basil sprigs.

Chicken and Shiitake Mushrooms

25 minutes to the table

SERVES 4

ingredients

MARINADE

generous ¾ cup sugar

1 cup soy sauce

1 tsp Chinese five-spice powder

1 cup sweet sherry

STIR-FRY

2 tbsp vegetable oil

1 lb 8 oz/675 g boneless chicken breast, skinned and cut into 1-inch/2.5-cm chunks

1 tsp grated fresh gingerroot

3 carrots, thinly sliced

2 onions, thinly sliced

⅔ cup fresh bean sprouts

8 oz/225 g shiitake mushrooms, thinly sliced

3 tbsp chopped fresh cilantro

boiled noodles, to serve

method

Put all the marinade ingredients in a bowl and mix well. Set aside until required.

Heat the oil in a preheated wok or large skillet over medium-high heat. Add the chicken and stir-fry for 2 minutes, then add the ginger and stir-fry for 1 minute. Add the marinade and cook, stirring, for an additional 2 minutes.

Add the carrots, onions, bean sprouts, mushrooms, and cilantro, one vegetable at a time and stir-fry for 30 seconds after each addition.

Once the marinade has reduced and thickened, transfer the stir-fry to warmed serving bowls. Serve hot with boiled noodles.

Red Curry Pork with Bell Peppers

25 minutes to the table

method

Heat the oil in a preheated wok or large skillet over medium-high heat. Add the onion and garlic and stir-fry for 1-2 minutes, or until soft but not brown.

Add the pork slices and stir-fry for 2-3 minutes, or until browned all over. Add the red bell pepper, mushrooms, and curry paste.

Meanwhile, dissolve the coconut in a bowl of hot stock. Add to the pan with the soy sauce. Bring to a boil, then reduce the heat and simmer for 4-5 minutes, or until the liquid has reduced and thickened.

Add the tomatoes and cilantro and cook, stirring, for 1-2 minutes before serving.

cook's tip

To skin tomatoes, cut a small cross in the bottom of each tomato with a sharp knife. Put in a heatproof bowl, then cover with boiling water and let stand for a minute or so. Remove with a slotted spoon and plunge into cold water. Drain and peel off the skins.

SERVES 4-6

ingredients

2 tbsp vegetable oil or peanut oil

1 onion, coarsely chopped

2 garlic cloves, chopped

1 lb/450 g pork tenderloin, thickly sliced

1 red bell pepper, seeded and cut into squares

6 oz/175 g mushrooms, cut into fourths

2 tbsp red Thai curry paste

4 oz/115 g creamed coconut, chopped

1¼ cups hot pork stock or vegetable stock

2 tbsp Thai soy sauce

4 tomatoes, skinned (see cook's tip), seeded, and chopped

handful of fresh cilantro, chopped

Surf 'n' Turf Skewers
25 minutes to the table

SERVES 2

ingredients

8 oz/225 g tenderloin steak,
    about 1 inch/2.5 cm thick
8 raw jumbo shrimp, shelled and
    deveined
olive oil, for oiling
4 tbsp butter
2 garlic cloves, crushed
3 tbsp chopped fresh parsley, plus
    extra sprigs to garnish
finely grated zest and juice of 1 lime
salt and pepper
lime wedges, to garnish
crusty bread, to serve

method

Cut the steak into 1-inch/2.5-cm cubes.

Thread an equal number of the steak cubes and shrimp onto 4 oiled flat metal kabob skewers or presoaked wooden skewers. Season the kabobs to taste with pepper.

Preheat the broiler to medium. Meanwhile, put half the butter and garlic in a small pan and heat gently until melted. Remove from the heat and add half the parsley, lime zest and juice, and salt and pepper to taste.

Brush the kabobs with some of the flavored butter. Put the kabobs on an oiled broiler rack and cook under the preheated broiler for 4–8 minutes, or until the steak is cooked according to your taste and the shrimp turn pink, turning the kabobs frequently during cooking and brushing with the remaining flavored butter halfway through cooking.

Meanwhile, melt the remaining butter with the garlic in a separate small pan, then remove from the heat and add the remaining parsley and lime zest and juice with salt and pepper to taste. Serve the kabobs hot on the skewers, with the flavored butter spooned over. Garnish with lime wedges and parsley sprigs, and serve with crusty bread to soak up the buttery juices.

Grilled Steak with Tomatoes and Garlic

25 minutes to the table

SERVES 4

ingredients

3 tbsp olive oil, plus extra
for brushing

1 lb 9 oz/700 g tomatoes, skinned
(see cook's tip) and chopped

1 red bell pepper, seeded and chopped

1 onion, chopped

2 garlic cloves, finely chopped

1 tbsp chopped fresh flat-leaf parsley

1 tsp dried oregano

1 tsp sugar

4 sirloin or round steaks, about
6 oz/175 g each

salt and pepper

method

Put the oil, tomatoes, red bell pepper, onion, garlic, parsley, oregano, and sugar in a heavy-bottomed pan and season to taste with salt and pepper. Bring to a boil, then reduce the heat and simmer, uncovered, for 15 minutes.

Meanwhile, preheat a grill pan over high heat. Snip any fat around the outsides of the steaks. Season each steak generously with pepper (no salt) and brush with oil. When the grill pan is very hot, add the steaks and cook for 1 minute on each side. Reduce the heat to medium and cook according to taste: 1½–2 minutes on each side for rare; 2½–3 minutes on each side for medium; or 3–4 minutes on each side for well done.

Transfer the steaks to warmed individual plates and spoon the sauce over. Serve immediately.

cook's tip

To peel tomatoes, cut a small cross in the base of each tomato with a sharp knife. Put in a heatproof bowl, then cover with boiling water and let stand for a minute or so. Remove with a slotted spoon and plunge into cold water. Drain and peel off the skins.

Mussels with Fennel
25 minutes to the table

method

Heat the oil in a large, heavy-bottomed pan or stockpot over medium-high heat. Add the onions and fennel and cook, stirring, for 3 minutes. Add the garlic and cook, stirring, for an additional 2 minutes, or until the onions and fennel are soft but not brown.

Add the wine and sherry and let bubble until reduced by half. Add the tomatoes with their juices and bring to a boil, stirring. Add the sugar and salt and pepper to taste, then reduce the heat and simmer, uncovered, for 5 minutes.

Meanwhile, clean the mussels by scrubbing or scraping the shells and pulling out any beards that are attached to them. Discard any with broken shells or any that refuse to close when tapped.

Reduce the heat under the pan to very low. Add the mussels, then cover and simmer, shaking the pan frequently, for 4 minutes, or until the mussels are opened. Discard any mussels that remain closed. Lift out the remaining mussels from the pan and divide between 4 serving bowls. Re-cover the pan and simmer the juices for an additional minute.

Stir the parsley into the juices in the pan. Taste and adjust the seasoning. Pour the juices over the bowls of mussels, and serve immediately with plenty of bread for soaking up the juices.

SERVES 4–6

ingredients

4 tbsp olive oil
2 large onions, thinly sliced
1 fennel bulb, thinly sliced
2 large garlic cloves, finely chopped
1½ cups dry white wine
scant ½ cup fino sherry
14 oz/400 g canned tomatoes
pinch of sugar
4 lb 8 oz/2 kg live mussels
handful of fresh parsley, finely
    chopped
salt and pepper
crusty bread, to serve

Salmon with Watercress Cream

25 minutes to the table

SERVES 4

ingredients

2 tbsp unsalted butter

1 tbsp sunflower-seed or corn oil

4 salmon fillets, about 6 oz/175 g
    each, skinned

SAUCE

1¼ cups sour cream

2 tbsp snipped fresh dill

1 garlic clove, finely chopped

scant ½ cup dry white wine

bunch of watercress, finely chopped,
    with a few sprigs reserved for
    garnish

salt and pepper

method

For the sauce, pour the sour cream into a large, heavy-bottom pan and heat gently to simmering point. Remove from the heat, then stir in the dill and set aside until required.

Meanwhile, preheat a slow oven (325°F/160°C). Melt the butter with the oil in a heavy-bottomed skillet. Add the salmon fillets and cook over medium heat for 4–5 minutes on each side, or until cooked through. Remove the fish from the skillet, then cover and keep warm in the slow oven.

Add the garlic to the skillet and cook, stirring, for 1 minute. Pour in the wine, then bring to a boil and cook until reduced. Stir the sour cream mixture into the skillet and cook for 2–3 minutes, or until thickened.

Stir in the watercress and cook until just wilted. Season to taste with salt and pepper. Put the salmon fillets on warmed serving plates and spoon over the watercress sauce, then garnish with the reserved watercress sprigs and serve immediately.

variation

If watercress is unavailable, then replace with the same amount of arugula or baby spinach leaves.

Italian Sardines
30 minutes to the table

SERVES 4

ingredients

1 tbsp olive oil

4 garlic cloves, coarsely chopped

1 lb 7 oz/650 g fresh sardines, cleaned
and scaled (see cook's tip)

grated zest of 2 lemons

2 tbsp chopped fresh
flat-leaf parsley

salt and pepper

tomato, onion, and chive salad,
to serve

BRUSCHETTA

4 thick slices ciabatta or
other rustic bread

2 garlic cloves, halved

2 large tomatoes, halved

method

Preheat the broiler to medium. Heat the oil in a large, heavy-bottomed skillet. Add the chopped garlic and cook over low heat, stirring frequently, until soft.

For the bruschetta, lightly toast the bread on both sides under the preheated broiler. Keep warm in a low oven.

Add the sardines to the skillet and cook for 5 minutes, turning once. Sprinkle with the lemon zest and parsley and season to taste with salt and pepper.

Meanwhile, to finish the bruschetta, rub one side of each slice of toast with the cut side of a garlic clove half, then with the cut side of a tomato half. Divide the bruschetta and sardines between 4 serving plates and serve immediately with a tomato, onion, and chive salad.

cook's tip

To clean the sardines, slit open the belly and remove the insides. Rinse and dry. To scale, hold each fish in turn by its tail under cold running water and run your hand along the body from tail to head until the scales are removed.

Red Snapper with Fennel and Bell Peppers

25 minutes to the table

method

Pick over the snapper fillets and use a pair of tweezers to remove any fine bones running down the center of each fillet.

Heat half the oil in a large sauté pan or skillet with a tight-fitting lid over medium-high heat. Add the red bell peppers, fennel, and garlic, and stir well. Add salt and pepper to taste. Reduce the heat to medium-low, then cover and cook for 15–20 minutes, or until soft.

Meanwhile, preheat the broiler to high. When the broiler is very, very hot, brush the skin of the fillets with some of the remaining oil and season to taste with salt and pepper. Put the fillets on a baking sheet skin-side up, and cook under the preheated broiler for 3 minutes, or until the skin crisps and turns golden brown.

Turn the fillets over, then brush again with the remaining oil and season to taste with salt and pepper. Cook for an additional minute or so until the flesh flakes easily when tested with the tip of a knife.

Divide the fennel and bell peppers equally between 4 plates. Cut each fillet in half and arrange 3 halves on top of each portion of vegetables. Serve immediately with lemon wedges for squeezing over, if desired.

cook's tip

To avoid the messy business of removing the fine bones from the fish and to save time, ask your fish-dealer to do it for you.

SERVES 4

ingredients

6 red snapper fillets, about 4½ oz/
    125 g each, scaled (see cook's tip)
4 tbsp olive oil
2 large red bell peppers, seeded and
    thinly sliced
2 fennel bulbs, thinly sliced
2 large garlic cloves, crushed
salt and pepper
lemon wedges, to serve (optional)

Fusilli with Gorgonzola and Mushroom Sauce

20 minutes to the table

SERVES 4

ingredients

3 cups dried fusilli

3 tbsp olive oil

12 oz/350 g wild mushrooms (see cook's tip), sliced

1 garlic clove, finely chopped

1¾ cups heavy cream

9 oz/250 g Gorgonzola cheese, crumbled

salt and pepper

2 tbsp chopped fresh flat-leaf parsley, to garnish

method

Bring a large pan of lightly salted water to a boil. Add the pasta, then return to a boil and cook according to the package directions, until tender but still firm to the bite.

Meanwhile, heat the oil in a large, heavy-bottomed pan over low heat. Add the mushrooms and cook, stirring frequently, for 5 minutes. Add the garlic and cook, stirring, for an additional 2 minutes.

Add the cream, then bring to a boil and cook for 1 minute, or until slightly thickened. Stir in the cheese and cook over low heat until it has melted. Do not let the sauce boil once the cheese has been added. Season to taste with salt and pepper and remove from the heat.

Drain the pasta and add to the sauce. Toss well to coat, then serve immediately, garnished with the parsley.

cook's tip

Wild mushrooms have a much earthier flavor than cultivated ones, so they complement the strong taste of the cheese. Porcini are especially delicious, but rather expensive. Portobello or Caesar's mushrooms, if you can find them, would also be a good choice. Otherwise, use cultivated mushrooms, but add 1 oz/25 g dried porcini, presoaked for 20 minutes in 1 cup hot water.

Vermicelli with Vegetable Ribbons

20 minutes to the table

SERVES 4

ingredients

12 oz/350 g dried vermicelli

3 carrots

3 zucchini

2 tbsp unsalted butter

1 tbsp olive oil

2 garlic cloves, finely chopped

3 oz/85 g fresh basil, shredded

1 oz/25 g fresh chives, finely snipped

1 oz/25 g fresh flat-leaf parsley, finely
    chopped

1 small head of radicchio, leaves
    shredded

salt and pepper

method

Bring a large pan of lightly salted water to a boil. Add the pasta, then return to a boil and cook according to the package directions, until tender but still firm to the bite.

Meanwhile, using a swivel-bladed vegetable peeler or a mandoline (see cook's tip), cut the zucchini and carrots into very thin strips. Melt the butter with the oil in a heavy-bottomed skillet. Add the carrot strips and garlic and cook over low heat, stirring occasionally, for 5 minutes. Add the zucchini strips and all the herbs and season to taste with salt and pepper.

Drain the pasta and add to the skillet. Toss well to mix and cook briefly, stirring. Transfer to a warmed serving dish. Add the radicchio, then toss well and serve immediately.

variation

If desired, you can garnish the dish with thin fresh shavings of Parmesan cheese or crumbled feta cheese.

cook's tip

A mandoline is a cook's gadget that predates the food processor and chops and slices with ease. It usually has adjustable blades that make it easy to cut shapes such as thin slices, short thin sticks, or strands.

Sweet-and-Sour Vegetables with Cashews

20 minutes to the table

method

Heat both the oils in a preheated wok or large skillet over high heat. Add the onions and stir-fry for 1–2 minutes, or until beginning to soften.

Add the carrots, zucchini, and broccoli, and stir-fry for 2–3 minutes. Add the mushrooms, bok choy, jaggery, soy sauce, and vinegar, and stir-fry for 1–2 minutes.

Meanwhile, toast the cashews in a dry skillet. Sprinkle over the stir-fry and serve immediately.

SERVES 4

ingredients

1 tbsp vegetable oil or peanut oil

1 tsp chili oil

2 onions, sliced

2 carrots, thinly sliced

2 zucchini, thinly sliced

4 oz/115 g head broccoli, cut into florets

4 oz/115 g white mushrooms, sliced

4 oz/115 g small bok choy, halved

2 tbsp jaggery or soft light brown sugar

2 tbsp Thai soy sauce

1 tbsp rice vinegar

generous ⅓ cup raw unsalted cashews

Chapter Three
Salads

Artichoke and Arugula Salad

20 minutes to the table

SERVES 4

ingredients

8 baby globe artichokes
juice of 2 lemons
bunch of arugula, washed and dried
½ cup extra-virgin olive oil
4 oz/115 g romano cheese
salt and pepper

method

Break off the stems of the artichokes and cut off about 1 inch/2.5 cm of the tops, depending on how young and small they are. Remove and discard any coarse outer leaves, leaving only the pale, tender inner leaves. Use a teaspoon to scoop out and remove the chokes, which are inedible. Rub each artichoke with a little of the lemon juice as soon as it is prepared to prevent it from discoloring.

Thinly slice the artichokes and put in a salad bowl. Add the arugula, remaining lemon juice, and oil, then season to taste with salt and pepper and toss together.

Using a swivel-bladed vegetable peeler, thinly shave the romano cheese over the salad, then serve immediately.

variation

If only larger artichokes are available, cook them in a pan of lightly salted boiling water for 15 minutes, then refresh under cold running water before slicing.

Fava Bean Salad
25 minutes to the table

SERVES 4

ingredients

3 lb/1.3 kg shelled fresh young fava
    beans or 1 lb 8 oz/675 g frozen
    baby fava beans
5½ oz/150 g authentic Greek feta
    cheese (drained weight)
bunch of scallions, thinly sliced
2 tbsp chopped fresh dill or mint (see
    cook's tip)
2 hard-cooked eggs, shelled and cut
    into fourths
pepper

DRESSING

6 tbsp extra-virgin olive oil
grated zest of 1 lemon and 2 tbsp
    freshly squeezed lemon juice
1 small garlic clove, crushed
pinch of sugar

TO SERVE

lemon wedges
strained plain yogurt (optional)

method

Make the dressing by whisking the oil, lemon zest and juice, garlic, sugar, and pepper to taste, together in a small bowl. Set aside until required.

Shell the fresh fava beans, if using, and cook in a pan of boiling salted water for 5–10 minutes, or until tender. If using frozen fava beans, cook in a pan of boiling salted water for 4–5 minutes, or until tender. Drain the cooked beans and put in a salad bowl.

Whisk the dressing and pour over the beans while they are still warm. Crumble over the feta cheese, then add the scallions and toss together. Sprinkle over the dill and arrange the egg quarters around the edge.

Serve warm with lemon wedges, and a bowl of strained plain yogurt to spoon on top, if you wish.

cook's tip

If using mint in this salad, sprinkle a pinch of sugar over it as you chop, to bring out its full aroma.

Salad of Greens with Lemon Dressing

10 minutes to the table

method

Wash the salad greens in cold water and discard any thick stems. Pat dry with paper towels and put in a salad bowl. Add the herbs.

Make the dressing by whisking the oil, lemon juice, garlic, and salt and pepper to taste together in a small bowl. Taste and add more oil or lemon juice if necessary.

Just before serving, whisk the dressing, then pour over the salad greens and toss together. Serve immediately.

SERVES 4

ingredients

7 oz/200 g mixed baby salad greens, such as mâche, spinach, watercress, and arugula
4 tbsp chopped fresh mixed herbs, such as flat-leaf parsley, mint, cilantro, and basil

DRESSING

about 4 tbsp extra-virgin olive oil
juice of about ½ lemon
1 garlic clove, crushed
salt and pepper

Traditional Greek Salad
15 minutes to the table

SERVES 4

ingredients

7 oz/200 g authentic Greek feta
   cheese (drained weight)
½ head iceberg lettuce or 1 lettuce
   such as romaine or escarole,
   shredded or sliced
4 tomatoes, cut into fourths
½ cucumber, sliced
12 Greek black olives
2 tbsp chopped fresh herbs, such
   as oregano, flat-leaf parsley, mint,
   or basil

DRESSING

6 tbsp extra-virgin olive oil
2 tbsp freshly squeezed lemon juice
1 garlic clove, crushed
pinch of sugar
salt and pepper

method

Make the dressing by whisking the oil, lemon juice, garlic, sugar, and salt and pepper to taste, in a small bowl. Set aside until required.

Cut the feta cheese into 1-inch/2.5-cm cubes. Put the lettuce, tomatoes, and cucumber in a salad bowl. Scatter over the cheese and toss together.

Just before serving, whisk the dressing, then pour over the salad greens and toss together. Scatter over the olives and chopped herbs and serve immediately.

Corn Salad and Beets

10 minutes to the table

SERVES 4

ingredients

6 oz/175 g corn salad

4 small cooked beets, diced

2 tbsp chopped walnuts

DRESSING

2 tbsp freshly squeezed lemon juice

2 garlic cloves, finely chopped

1 tbsp Dijon mustard

pinch of sugar

½ cup sunflower-seed or corn oil

½ cup sour cream

salt and pepper

method

Make the dressing by whisking the lemon juice, garlic, mustard, sugar, and salt and pepper to taste, in a bowl. Gradually whisk in the oil. Lightly beat the sour cream, then whisk it into the dressing.

Put the corn salad in a bowl and pour over one-third of the dressing. Toss to coat.

Divide the lettuce equally between 4 individual bowls. Top each portion with an equal quantity of beet and drizzle with the remaining dressing. Sprinkle with the walnuts and serve immediately.

cook's tip

You can prepare the dressing in advance, but do not add it to the salad until you are ready to serve, otherwise the greens will become soggy.

Julienne Vegetable Salad

20 minutes to the table

method

Preheat a slow oven (325°F/160°C). Heat the oil in a preheated wok or large skillet over high heat. Add the bean curd and stir-fry for 3–4 minutes, or until browned all over. Remove with a slotted spoon, then drain on paper towels and keep warm in the preheated oven.

Add the red onion and scallions, garlic, and carrots to the wok, and stir-fry for 1–2 minutes. Add all the remaining vegetables, except the bean sprouts, and stir-fry for 2–3 minutes. Add the bean sprouts, then stir in the curry paste, soy sauce, vinegar, jaggery, and basil leaves, and cook, stirring, for 30 seconds.

Meanwhile, soak the noodles in a heatproof bowl or pan of boiling water or stock for 2–3 minutes, or according to the package directions, until tender. Drain well.

Divide the noodles equally between 4 individual bowls. Pile the vegetables onto the noodles and top with the tofu cubes. Garnish with extra basil, if desired, and serve immediately.

SERVES 4

ingredients

4 tbsp vegetable oil or peanut oil

8 oz/225 g bean curd with herbs
   (drained weight), cubed

1 red onion, sliced

4 scallions, cut into 2-inch/5-cm
   lengths

1 garlic clove, chopped

2 carrots, cut into short thin sticks

4 oz/115 g fine green beans, trimmed

1 yellow bell pepper, seeded and
   cut into strips

4 oz/115 g head broccoli,
   cut into florets

1 large zucchini, cut into short thin
   sticks

⅓ cup fresh bean sprouts

2 tbsp Thai red curry paste

4 tbsp Thai soy sauce

1 tbsp rice vinegar

1 tsp jaggery or soft light brown sugar

few fresh Thai basil leaves, plus extra
   to garnish (optional)

12 oz/350 g rice vermicelli noodles

Raspberry and Feta Salad with Couscous

20 minutes to the table

SERVES 6

ingredients

12 oz/350 g couscous

2½ cups boiling chicken stock or
    vegetable stock

12 oz/350 g fresh raspberries

8 oz/225 g feta cheese (drained
    weight), cubed or crumbled

2 zucchini, thinly sliced

4 scallions, diagonally sliced

⅓ cup pine nuts, toasted

small bunch of fresh basil, shredded

grated zest of 1 lemon

DRESSING

1 tbsp white wine vinegar

1 tbsp balsamic vinegar

4 tbsp extra-virgin olive oil

juice of 1 lemon

salt and pepper

method

Put the couscous in a large, heatproof bowl and pour over the stock. Stir well, then cover and let soak until all the stock has been absorbed.

Meanwhile, pick over the raspberries, discarding any that are overripe.

Transfer the couscous to a large serving bowl and stir well to break up any lumps. Add the feta cheese, zucchini, scallions, raspberries, and pine nuts. Stir in the shredded basil and lemon zest and gently toss all the ingredients together.

Put all the dressing ingredients in a screw-top jar, with salt and pepper to taste, then screw on the lid and shake until well blended. Pour over the salad and serve immediately.

Quinoa Salad

25 minutes to the table

SERVES 4

ingredients

6 oz/175 g quinoa

2½ cups water

10 vine-ripened cherry tomatoes,
    seeded and chopped

3-inch/7.5-cm piece cucumber, diced

3 scallions, finely chopped

juice of ½ lemon

2 tbsp extra-virgin olive oil

4 tbsp chopped fresh mint

4 tbsp chopped fresh cilantro

4 tbsp chopped fresh parsley

salt and pepper

method

Put the quinoa in a medium-size pan and cover with the water. Bring to a boil, then reduce the heat and simmer, covered, over low heat for 15 minutes. Drain if necessary.

Let the quinoa cool slightly before combining with the remaining ingredients in a salad bowl. Season to taste with salt and pepper. Serve at room temperature.

variation

The super-nutritious grain quinoa is featured in this recipe, but bulgur wheat or couscous can be used instead.

Orange and Fennel Salad

20 minutes to the table

method

Finely grate the zest from the oranges into a bowl and set aside. Using a small, serrated knife and working over a bowl to catch the juice, remove all the white pith from the oranges. Cut the oranges horizontally into thin slices.

Toss the orange slices with the fennel and onion slices in a salad bowl. Whisk the oil into the reserved orange juice, then spoon over the salad. Scatter the olive slices over the top. Add the chile, if using, then sprinkle with the orange zest. Garnish with parsley and serve immediately with French bread.

variations

Garnet-red blood oranges look stunning in this salad. Juicy dark grapes make an interesting alternative to the olives.

SERVES 4

ingredients

4 large juicy oranges
1 large fennel bulb, very thinly sliced
1 mild white onion, thinly sliced
2 tbsp extra-virgin olive oil
12 plump black olives, pitted and thinly sliced
1 fresh red chile, seeded and very thinly sliced (optional)
finely chopped fresh parsley, to garnish
French bread, to serve

Spinach and Garlic Salad

25 minutes to the table

SERVES 4

ingredients

12 garlic cloves, unpeeled

4 tbsp olive oil

1 lb/450 g baby spinach leaves,
  washed and dried

½ cup chopped walnuts or
  generous ⅓ cup pine nuts

2 tbsp freshly squeezed lemon juice

salt and pepper

method

Preheat the oven to 375°F/190°C. Put the garlic cloves in an ovenproof dish, then add half the oil and toss to coat. Roast in the preheated oven for 15 minutes.

Transfer the garlic and oil to a salad bowl. Add the spinach leaves, walnuts, lemon juice, and remaining oil. Toss well together and season to taste with salt and pepper.

Transfer the salad to individual dishes and serve immediately, while the garlic is still warm. Diners can squeeze the softened garlic out of the skins at the table.

variation

Substitute young sorrel leaves for the baby spinach leaves to give this salad a delicious citrus flavor.

Chapter Four
Desserts

Broiled Honeyed Figs with Sabayon

15 minutes to the table

SERVES 4

ingredients

8 ripe fresh figs, halved

4 tbsp clear honey

leaves from 2 fresh rosemary sprigs,
    finely chopped (optional)

3 eggs

method

Preheat the broiler to high. Arrange the figs, cut-side up, on the broiler rack. Brush with half the honey, and scatter over the rosemary, if using.

Cook under the preheated broiler for 5–6 minutes, or until just beginning to caramelize.

Meanwhile, to make the sabayon, lightly whisk the eggs with the remaining honey in a large, heatproof bowl, then set over a pan of simmering water. Using a hand-held electric whisk, beat the eggs and honey together for 10 minutes, or until pale and thick.

Put 4 fig halves on each of 4 serving plates, then add a generous spoonful of the sabayon and serve immediately.

caution

Recipes using raw or lightly cooked eggs should be avoided by infants, the elderly, pregnant women, convalescents, and anyone suffering from an illness.

Grilled Bananas

20 minutes to the table

SERVES 4

ingredients

2 oz/55 g creamed coconut, chopped

⅔ cup heavy cream

4 bananas

juice and finely grated zest of 1 lime,
   plus 1 lime, cut into wedges

1 tbsp vegetable oil or peanut oil

½ cup dry unsweetened coconut

method

Put the creamed coconut and cream in a small pan and heat over low heat until the coconut has dissolved. Remove from the heat and let cool for 10 minutes, then whisk until thick but floppy.

Preheat a grill pan over high heat. Peel the bananas and toss in the lime juice and zest. Brush the preheated grill pan with the oil, then add the bananas and cook, turning once, for 2–3 minutes, or until soft and brown. Add the lime wedges halfway through the cooking time.

Meanwhile, preheat the broiler to medium. Toast the dry unsweetened coconut on a piece of foil under the preheated broiler until lightly browned. Serve the bananas with the lime wedges and coconut cream, sprinkled with the broiled coconut.

Nectarine Crunch
10 minutes to the table

method

Using a sharp knife, cut the nectarines in half, then remove and discard the pits. Chop the flesh into bite-size pieces. Reserve a few pieces for decoration and put a few of the remaining pieces in the bottom of 3 sundae glasses. Put a layer of oat cereal in each glass, then drizzle over a little of the yogurt.

Put the preserve and peach nectar in a large pitcher and stir together to mix. Add a few more nectarine pieces to the glasses and drizzle over a little of the preserve. Continue building up the layers in this way, finishing with a layer of yogurt and a sprinkling of oat cereal. Decorate with the reserved nectarine pieces and serve.

cook's tip

There is no need to peel the nectarines—just wash and pat dry with paper towels.

SERVES 3

ingredients

4 nectarines
6 oz/175 g raisin and nut crunchy
   oat cereal
1¼ cups lowfat plain yogurt
2 tbsp peach preserve
2 tbsp peach nectar

Mixed Fruit Brûlées
20 minutes to the table

SERVES 4

ingredients

1 lb/450 g prepared assorted summer
   fruit, such as strawberries,
   raspberries, black currants, red
   currants, and cherries, thawed
   if frozen
⅓ cup sour cream
⅓ cup mascarpone
1 tsp vanilla extract
4 tbsp raw brown sugar

method

Preheat the broiler to medium. Divide the prepared fruit equally
between 4 small ramekin dishes.

Combine the sour cream, mascarpone, and vanilla extract in a bowl.
Spoon the mixture over the fruit to cover it completely.

Top each serving with 1 tablespoon of raw brown sugar. Cook the
desserts under the preheated broiler until the sugar is beginning to
caramelize. Set aside for a couple of minutes before serving.

variations

For a richer result, use lightly whipped full-fat or half-fat light or heavy
cream instead of the sour cream and mascarpone. Alternatively, for an
even lower-fat version, use all mascarpone.

Baked Peaches
20 minutes to the table

SERVES 4

ingredients

4 large ripe fresh peaches
1 oz/25 g dried apricots, finely
    chopped
1 oz/25 g fresh blueberries
1 tbsp slivered almonds, toasted
2 tbsp medium sherry or orange juice
mascarpone or frozen yogurt,
    to serve

method

Preheat the oven to 350°F/180°C.

If preferred, skin the peaches. To do this, cut a small cross in the bottom of each peach with a sharp knife. Put in a large, heatproof bowl, then cover with boiling water and let stand for 2 minutes. Remove with a slotted spoon and plunge into cold water. Drain and remove the skins.

Cut the peaches in half and remove and discard the pits.

Put in an ovenproof dish with the peach pit cavity facing up.

Put the apricots in a bowl with the blueberries and stir together. Divide the fruit mixture equally between the peach pit cavities. Sprinkle with the almonds.

Pour over the sherry, then bake in the preheated oven for 10 minutes, or until heated through. Serve with mascarpone or frozen yogurt.

Peaches with Raspberry Sauce
20 minutes to the table

method

Puree the raspberries in a food processor or blender, then press through a fine nonmetallic strainer into a bowl to remove the seeds.

Stir the orange zest and juice and the liqueur into the raspberry puree. Add sugar to taste, stirring until the sugar dissolves. Cover and let chill in the refrigerator until required.

Skin the peaches. To do this, cut a small cross in the bottom of each peach with a sharp knife. Put in a large, heatproof bowl, then cover with boiling water and let stand for 2 minutes. Remove with a slotted spoon and plunge into cold water. Drain and peel off the skins. Cut the peaches in half and discard the pits.

Cut each peach half into fourths and stir into the raspberry sauce. Cover and let chill in the refrigerator until required.

When ready to serve, put 1-2 scoops of ice cream into individual glasses or bowls, then top with the peaches and spoon over some extra sauce. Serve with cats' tongue cookies on the side, if desired.

cook's tip

When fresh raspberries are not in season, use frozen ones.

SERVES 4-6

ingredients

1 lb/450 g fresh raspberries (see cook's tip)
finely grated zest of 1 orange
2 tbsp freshly squeezed orange juice
2 tbsp Grand Marnier, Cointreau, or other orange-flavored liqueur
2-3 tbsp superfine sugar
6 ripe fresh peaches

TO SERVE
vanilla ice cream
cats' tongue cookies (optional)

Broiled Cinnamon Oranges

10 minutes to the table

SERVES 6

ingredients

4 large oranges

1 tsp ground cinnamon

1 tbsp raw brown sugar

method

Preheat the broiler to high. Cut the oranges in half and discard any seeds. Using a sharp or curved grapefruit knife, carefully cut the flesh away from the skin by cutting around the edge of the fruit. Cut across the segments to loosen the flesh into bite-size pieces that will then spoon out easily.

Arrange the orange halves, cut-side up, in a shallow, flameproof dish. Mix the cinnamon with the sugar in a small bowl and sprinkle evenly over the orange halves.

Cook under the preheated broiler for 3–5 minutes, or until the sugar has caramelized and is golden and bubbling. Serve immediately.

Index